River

River

Poems by Ted Hughes
Photographs by Peter Keen

ff

faber and faber LONDON · BOSTON in association with JAMES & JAMES

First published in 1983
by Faber and Faber Limited
3 Queen Square London WC1N 3AU
In association with James & James
6 Rona Road London NW3 2JA
Colour origination by Wensum Graphics, Norwich
Printed in Great Britain by
Jolly & Barber Limited, Rugby
All rights reserved

British Library Cataloguing in Publication Data

Hughes, Ted
River.
1. Rivers—Poetry   2. English poetry
I. Title   II. Keen, Peter
821'.008'036   PR1195.R/

ISBN 0-571-13088-7
ISBN 0-571-13093-3 Pbk

The Countryside Commission is concerned to conserve and enhance the natural beauty and amenity of the countryside; and to secure public access for open-air recreation. The Commission replaced and assumed the functions of the National Parks Commission when the Countryside Act became law in 1968.

The British Gas Corporation has to 'develop and maintain an efficient, co-ordinated and economical system of gas supply'. Because the Corporation's major investment is in underground pipelines and rural installations, it has to achieve this primary objective with care, taking into account legislation such as the Countryside Act under which it must 'have regard to the desirability of conserving the natural beauty and amenity of the countryside'.

Over many years, British Gas has developed a very positive attitude to conserving the natural environment, and this policy has created an atmosphere of trust among those responsible for planning in local authorities and in the communities affected. As a result British Gas has been able to introduce a gas supply system which now carries well over one third of the heat energy used in Britain. This has been built during the past twenty years with only minor impact on the countryside.

Published with the assistance of British Gas and the Countryside Commission.

For Andrea and for Nicholas

Contents

The Morning Before Christmas

Buds fur-gloved with frost. Everything had come to a standstill
In a brand new stillness.
The river-trees, in a blue haze,
Were fractured domes of spun ghost.
Wheel-ruts frost-fixed. Mid-morning, slowly
The sun pushed dark spokes of melt and sparkle
Across the fields of hoar. And the river steamed –
Flint-olive.
            By the salmon-ladder at the weir –
The sluice cut, the board exit lifted –
The cage drained slowly. A dead cock fish
Hung its head into the leaf-dregs. Another
Sunk on its side, seemed to pincer-lock
The cage wire with its kipe. Already
They were slinging the dead out, rigid in the net,
Great, lolling lilies of fungus, irreplaceable –
Eggs rotten in them, milt rotten. Nothing
So raggy dead offal as a dead
Salmon in its wedding finery. So
After their freakish luck in the lottery –
Their five thousand to one against survival –
Dead within days of marriage. Three, four, five.

Then a hen fish – ten pounds – lurching alive.
Rough grip and her head in an armpit.
Now the thumb and finger kneading her belly.

The frost-smoking sun embellishes her beauty,
Her red-black love-paints, her helpless, noble mask.
Suddenly eggs
Squirt in a liquid loosening – spatter
Into the kitchen bowl. A long, deep-kneading
Oily massage – again and again. Then the fish
Drop-slung, head down, ponderous jerk-shake, and up
For another milking. And now, gentler,
An artful, back-of-the-fingers, cheek-stroke-dainty
Feathering along her flank sets the eggs spurting –
She tries to writhe and shiver a real mating.
The pink mess deepens in the bowl, and her belly
Starts to bag empty. Still there's more. Amazing
Finally the wealth of eggs. Then a cock –
Brindled black and crimson, with big, precious spots
Like a jeweller's trout – gapes his hook
And releases a milk-jet of sperm
Under a skilful thumb, into the treasure.
A little is plenty. He goes back into the net
And into the river – to wait
For his next violation. A stirring
Now of eggs and milt, to a vital broth.
Then they're set aside. Another hen-fish
Comes wagging weakly from the prison.
Four fish only, forty-odd thousand eggs.
The hard frosts this last week
Brought the fish on, ripened them, but killed
Five with sudden death-bloom. Six
Kicking strong, clean, green, unripe, refuse
To yield an egg to the handling. They go
Free above the weir – gloom-flag dissolve
Under the whorled, sliding, morning-smoking
Flat of the pool above. With luck

In natural times, those six, with luck,
In five years, with great luck, might make nine.

That's how four kitchen plastic bowls
Employ eight grown men and keep them solemn.
Precarious obstetrics. First, the eggs clot,
Then loosen. Then, lovingly, the rinsings,
The lavings, the drainings, the rewashings –
A few eggs trundle clear and vanish
Into the white crash of the weir.
                                        A world
Wrought in wet, heavy gold. Treasure-solid.
That morning
Dazzle-stamped every cell in my body
With its melting edge, its lime-bitter brightness.

A flood pond, inch-iced, held the moment of a fox
In touch-melted and refrozen dot-prints.

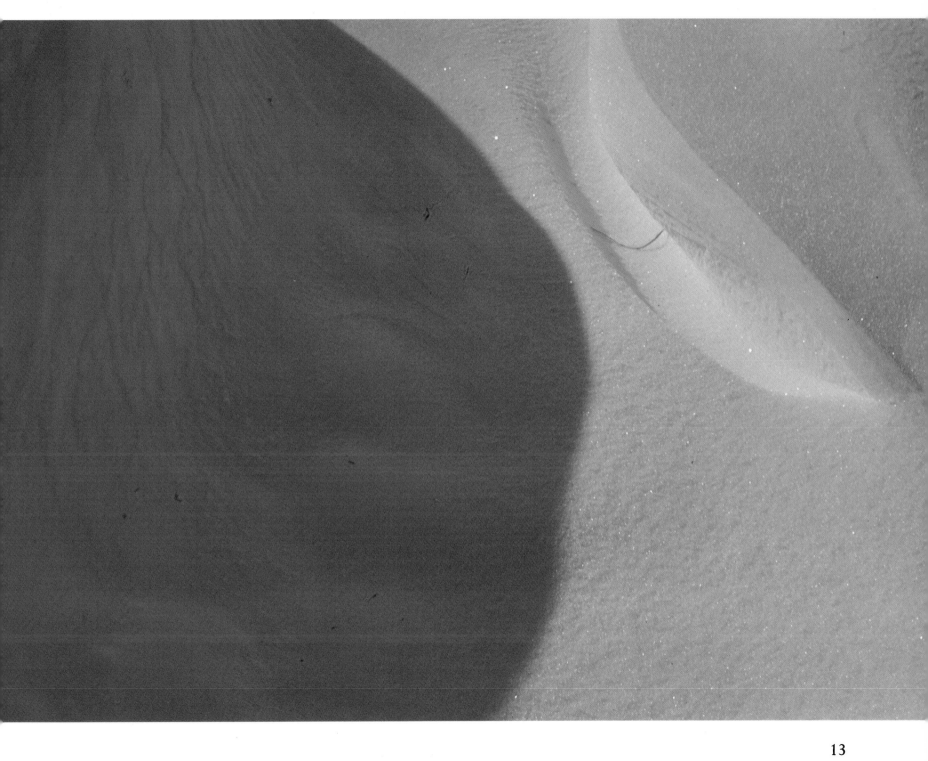

13

Japanese River Tales

1

Tonight
From the swaddled village, down the padded lane
Snow is hurrying
To the tryst, is touching
At her hair, at her raiment
Glint-slippered
Over the stubble,
                    naked under
Her light robe, jewels
In her hair, in her ears, at her bare throat
Dark eye-flash
              twigs and brambles
Catch at her
          as she lifts
The tattered curtains
Of the river's hovel, and plunges
Into his grasping bed.

2

The lithe river rejoices all morning
In his juicy bride – the snow princess
Who peeped from clouds, and chose him,
              and descended.

The tale goes on
With glittery laughter of immortals
Shaking the alders –
In the end a drowsy after-bliss
Blue-hazes the long valley. High gulls
Look down on the flash
And langour of suppled shoulders
Bedded in her ermine.
                  Night
Lifts off the illusion. Lifts
The beauty from her skull. The sockets, in fact,
Are root-arches – empty
To ashes of stars. Her kiss
Grips through the full throat and locks
On the dislodged vertebrae.
                  Her talons
Lengthened by moonlight, numb open
The long belly of blood.
                  And the river
Is a gutter of death,
A spill of glitters
              dangling from her grasp
As she flies
Through the shatter of space and
Out of being.

Flesh of Light

From a core-flash, from a thunder-silence
Inside the sun, the smelting
Crawls and glimmers among heather-topped stones.

The mill of the galaxy, the generator
Making the atoms dance
With its reverberations, brims out lowly

For cattle to wade. They lift muzzles
That unspool the glair,
Dark bodies dense with boiling light.

The power-line, alive in its rough trench,
Electrifies the anemones
And the bristling wheat. A chrism of birth

Anoints the earth's bones. Ferns, unfolding baby fists,
Nod into upreaching, eyes of egg-film
Wobble for focus, in the throbbing aura

Of the river's magnetic descent.
This is the sun's oiled snake, dangling, fallen,
The medicinal mercury creature

Sheathed with the garb, in all its inscribed scales,
That it sheds
And refreshes, spasming and whispering.

Spinal cord of the prone adoring land,
Rapt
To the roots of the sea, to the blossoming

Of the sea.

New Year

Snow falls on the salmon redds. Painful

To think of the river tonight – suffering itself.
I imagine a Caesarian,
The wound's hapless mouth, a vital loss
Under the taut mask, on the heaped bed.

The silent to-fro hurrying of nurses,
The bowed stillness of surgeons,
A trickling in the hush. The intent steel
Stitching the frothing womb, in its raw hole.

And walking in the morning in the blue glare of the ward
I shall feel in my head the anaesthetic,
The stiff gauze, the congealments. I shall see
The gouged patient sunk in her trough of coma –

The lank, dying fish. But not the ticking egg.

19

Whiteness

Walks the river at dawn.

The thorn-tree hiding its thorns
With too much and too fleshy perfume.

Thin water. Uneasy ghost.
Whorls clotted with petals.

Trout, like a hidden man's cough,
Slash under dripping roots.

Heron. Clang
Coiling its snake in heavy hurry
Hoists away, yanked away

Ceases to ponder the cuneiform
Under glass

Huge owl-lump of dawn
With wrong fittings, a parasol broken
Tumbles up into strong sky

Banks precariously, risks a look
A writhing unmade bedstead

Sets the blade between its shoulders
And hang-falls
Down a long aim

Dangles its reeds

Till it can see its own pale eyes
Suddenly shakes off cumbersome cloud
To anchor, tall,
An open question.

Now only the river nags to be elsewhere.

Four March Watercolours

I   Earth is just unsettling
Her first faint scents.
                              My shadow, soft-edged,
On drying, pale sand, among baby nettles,
Where floodwater whorled and sowed it.
                                        The blue
Is a daze of bubbly fire – naked
Ushering and nursing of electricity
With caressings of air. Earth,
Mud-stained, stands in sparkling beggary.
                                        Bergs of old snow-drifts
Still stubborn in shadows.
                              The river
Acts fishless. It is
Fully occupied with its callisthenics,
Its twistings and self-wrestlings. The pool by the concrete buttress
Has just repaired its intricate engine,
Now revs it full-bore, underground,
Under my footsole. Tries to split the foundations,
Running in, testing and testing.
                                        Spring is over there.
Tits exciting the dour oak. Cows soften their calls
Into the far, crumble-soft calling
Of ewes. The land hangs, tremulous.
It pays full attention to each crow-caw,
Turning full-face to the entering, widening,
Flame-cored, burrowing havoc of a jet. Wild, stumpy daffodils
Shiver under the shock wave.

23

2   Nearly a warmth
Edging this wind.
                      A skylark, solitary
Glittering high out
Over the buoyant up-boil – a spice-particle
From the tumbled-out, hump-backed,
Bursting bales of river.
                 Spring
Just hesitates. She can't quite
Say what she feels yet. She's numb and pale.
But she's here, and looking at everything – first morning
Of real convalescence.
                The river's hard at it,
Tries and tries to wash and revive
A bedraggle of dirty bones. Primitive, radical
Engine of earth's renewal. A solution
Of all dead ends – an all-out evacuation
To the sea. All debts
Of wings and fronds, of eyes, nectar, roots, hearts
Returning, cancelled, to solvency –
Back to the sea's big re-think.
                 While the fieldful of novelty lambs
Suns and sprawls, mid-morning,
High-headed, happy, supposing
Here is a goodness that will stay forever.
A bluetit de-rusts its ratchet. We trees,
We tall ones, sunning, somewhat mutilated,
Inured by one more winter
To this muddy, heedless earth, and to our scaly
Provisional bodies, relax,
Enjoy the fraternity of survival,
Even a hope of new leaf.

3   The river
Concentrates its work. Its wheels churn.
Foam at the pool-tail blazes tawny – thrashing
Tight blown flames.
Bleeding the valley older.

                          An inch of snow
Whitened last night and the world
Slipped back under. This morning
Touch-precarious snow
Fledged all complexities of trees
And perfected fields. By noon
The earth's absorbed it.

                    An ewe,
Steep-spined, is lowering herself
To the power-coils
Of the river's bulge, to replenish her udder.
And a big-thumbed buzzard swirls
To a stall
Over the wood-top opposite, mewing, now settling
Heavy with domestic purpose.

                        Clouds lift anchors. The world
Tries its weights. All these branches are jammed
Solid with confidences. A market of gossip.
A spider has found me.

4   The river-epic
Rehearses itself. Embellishes afresh and afresh
Each detail. Baroque superabundance.
Earth-mouth brimming. But the snow-melt
Is an invisible restraint. If there are salmon
Under it all, they are in coma. They are stones
Lodged among stones, sealed as fossils
Under the grained pressure. I look down onto the pour
Of melted chocolate. They look up
At a guttering lamp
Through a sand-storm boil of silt
That scratches their lidless eyes,
Fumes from their gill-petals. They have to toil,
Trapped face-workers, in their holes of position
Under the mountain of water.

                       Up here
A lightness breathes, a morning-sleep lightness –
A glow on the closed eyelids
Or seen through the wet cracks of eyelashes
A crammed and jostly pushing
Of crow-tended, buzzard-adjusted
Germination. Now only hour after hour
Of the sweating, speechless labour of trees –

And the long ropes of light
Hauling the river's cargo
The oldest commerce.

Dee

The hills locked in snow
Have locked up their springs. The shining paps
That nurse the river's plumpness
Are locked up.
And the North Star is frozen in its lock.

The expenditure of swift purity
Nevertheless goes on. But so thinly,
So meanly, and from such stale cellars
No fish will face it.
Somewhere the salmon have turned back into the sea.

So this is the majesty of the April Dee
When the snowdrops, pert and apart,
Domes of ice-light, deviants
From a world preoccupied with water,
Hurt into perfection, steal a summer
Out of the old, river-worried
Carcase of winter.

Nothing else dare or can
Pilfer from the shrunk, steely procession.

Nevertheless, the lit queenliness of snow hills,
The high, frozen bosom, wears this river
Like a peculiarly fine jewel.

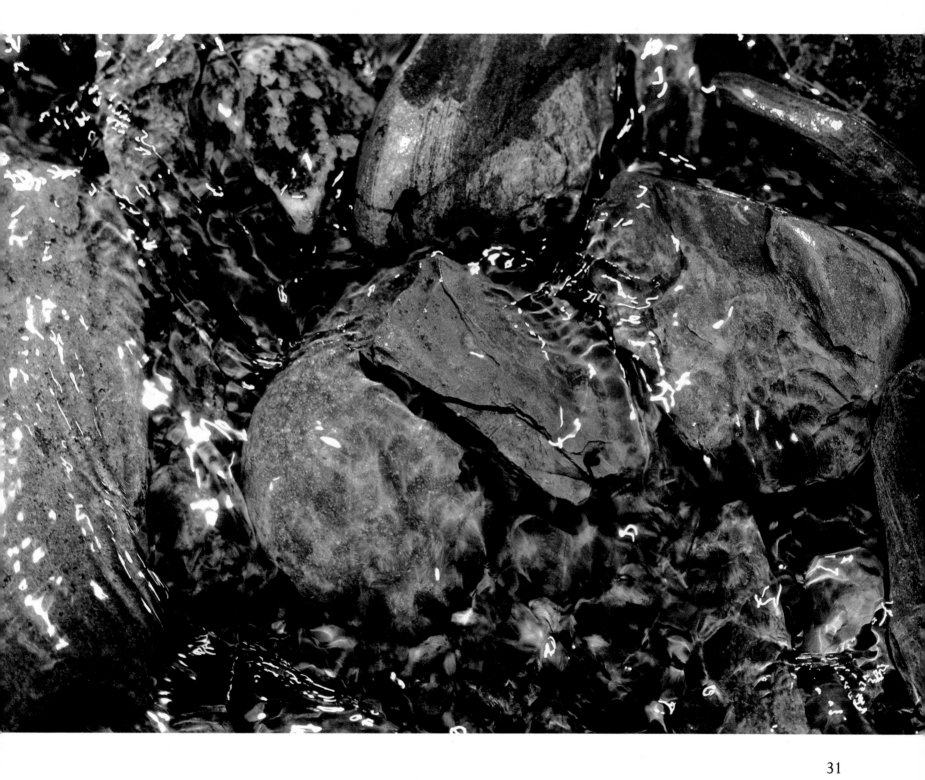

The Merry Mink

                    – the Arctic Indian's
Black bagful of hunter's medicine –
Now has to shift for himself.

Since he's here, he's decided to like it.
Now it is my turn, he says,
To enjoy my pelt uselessly.

I am the Mighty Northern Night, he says,
In my folktale form.
See, I leave my stars at the river's brim.

Little Black Thundercloud, lost from his mythology,
A-boil with lightnings
He can't get rid of. He romps through the ramsons

(Each one a constellation), topples into the river,
Jolly goblin, realist-optimist,
(Even his trapped, drowned snake-head grins)

As if he were deathless. Bobs up
Ruffed with a tough primaeval glee. Crams trout, nine together,
Into his bank-hole – his freezer –

Where they rot in three days. Makes love
Eight hours at a go.

                    My doings and my pelt,
He says, are a Platonic idea

Where I live with God.

Salmon-taking Times

After a routing flood-rain, the river
Was a sounder of wild muddy pigs
Flushed out of the hillsides. Tumbling hooligans
They jammed the old bends. Diabolical muscle,
Possessed sows and boars, frisk-tailed piglets,
Piling in the narrows.

                      I stayed clear. (''Swine
Bees and women cannot be turned.'')

                                But after
The warm shower
That just hazed and softened the daffodil buds
And clotted the primroses, a gauze
Struggles tenderly in the delighted current –
Clambers wetly on stones, and the river emerges
In glistenings, and gossamer bridal veils,
And hovers over itself – there is a wedding
Delicacy –
                        so delicate
I touch it and its beauty-frailty crumples
To a smear of wet, a strengthless wreckage
Of dissolving membranes – and the air is ringing.

It is like a religious moment, slightly dazing.

It is like a shower of petals of eglantine.

Under the Hill of Centurions

The river is in a resurrection fever.
Now at Easter you find them
Up in the pool's throat, and in the very jugular
Where the stickle pulses under grasses –

Cock minnows!

They have abandoned contemplation and prayer in the pool's crypt.

There they are, packed all together,
In an inch of seething light.

A stag-party, all bridegrooms, all in their panoply –

Red-breasted as if they bled,
Their bodies Roman bottle-glass green
Silked with black

In the clatter of the light loom of water
All singing and
Toiling together,
Wreathing their metals
Into the warp and weft of the lit water –

I imagine their song,
Deep-chested, striving, solemn.

A wrestling tress of kingfisher colour,
Steely jostlings, a washed mass of brilliants

Labouring at earth
In the wheel of light –

Ghostly rinsings
A struggle of spirits.

A Cormorant

Here before me, snake-head.
My waders weigh seven pounds.

My Barbour jacket, mainly necessary
For its pockets, is proof

Against the sky at my back. My bag
Sags with lures and hunter's medicine enough

For a year in the Pleistocene.
My hat, of use only

If this May relapses to March,
Embarrasses me, and my net, long as myself,

Optimistic, awkward, infatuated
With every twig-snag and fence-barb

Will slowly ruin the day. I paddle
Precariously on slimed shale,

And infiltrate twenty yards
Of gluey and magnetized spider-gleam

Into the elbowing dense jostle-traffic
Of the river's tunnel, and pray

With futuristic, archaic under-breath
So that some fish, telepathically overpowered,

Will attach its incomprehension
To the bauble I offer to space in general.

The cormorant eyes me, beak uptilted,
Body-snake low – sea-serpentish.

He's thinking: "Will that stump
Stay a stump just while I dive?" He dives.

He sheds everything from his tail end
Except fish-action, becomes fish,

Disappears from bird,
Dissolving himself

Into fish, so dissolving fish naturally
Into himself. Re-emerges, gorged,

Himself as he was, and escapes me.
Leaves me high and dry in my space-armour,

A deep-sea diver in two inches of water.

Stump Pool in April

Crack willows in their first pale eclosion
Of emerald. The long pool
Is simmering with oily lights. Deep labour
Embodied under filmy spanglings. Oxygen
Boils in its throat, and the new limbs
Flex and loosen. It keeps
Making the effort to burst its glistenings
With sinewy bulgings, gluey splittings
All down its living length.
                           The river is trying
To rise out of the river.
                April
Has set its lights working. Its broad wings
Creased and humped in their folds, convulse
To lift out over the daffodils.
                          The soft strokings
Of south wind keep touching all its membranes
Into spasming torments. It knows
The time has come for it to alter
And to fly, and somehow to tangle
With the hill-wood – waiting high there, flushed
In her bridal veil of haze violet.

Go Fishing

Join water, wade in underbeing
Let brain mist into moist earth
Ghost loosen away downstream
Gulp river and gravity

Lose words
Cease
Be assumed into the womb of lymph
As if creation were a wound
As if this flow were all plasm healing

Be supplanted by mud and leaves and pebbles
By sudden rainbow monster-structures
That materialise in suspension gulping
And dematerialise under pressure of the eye

Be cleft by the sliding prow
Displaced by the hull of light and shadow

Dissolved in earth-wave, the soft sun-shock,
Dismembered in sun-melt

Become translucent – one untangling drift
Of water-mesh, and a weight of earth-taste light
Mangled by wing-shadows
Everything circling and flowing and hover-still

Crawl out over roots, new and nameless
Search for face, harden into limbs

Let the world come back, like a white hospital
Busy with urgency words

Try to speak and nearly succeed
Heal into time and other people

Milesian Encounter on the Sligachan

For Hilary and Simon

"Up in the pools," they'd said, and "Two miles upstream."

Something sinister about bogland rivers.

And a shock —

> after the two miles of tumblequag, of Ice-Age
> hairiness, a crusty, quaking cadaver and me lurching
> over it in elation like a Daddylonglegs —
>
> after crooked little clatterbrook and again
> clatterbrook (a hurry of shallow grey light so
> distilled it looked like acid) —
>
> and after the wobbly levels of a razor-edged,
> blood-smeared grass, the flood-sucked swabs of bog-cotton,
> the dusty calico rip-up of snipe —
>
> under those petrified scapulae, vertebrae, horn-skulls
> the Cuillins (asylum of eagles) that were blue-silvered
> like wrinkled baking foil in the blue noon that day, and
> tremulous —
>
> early August, in a hot lateness (only three hours
> before my boat), a glance at my watch and suddenly

up to my hip in a suck-hole, then on again, teetering, over
the broken-necked heath-bobs, a good half-hour, and me
melting in my combined fuel of toil and clobber suddenly

The shock.
The sheer cavern of current piling silence
Under my feet.

So lonely-drowning deep, so drowned hair silent
So clear
Cleansing the body cavity of the underbog.

Such a brilliant cut-glass interior
Swinging under me.

And I felt a little bit giddy
Ghostly
As I fished the long pool tail
Peering into that superabundance of spirit.

And now where were they, my fellow-aliens from prehistory?
Those peculiar eyes
So like mine, but fixed at zero,
Searching in from space,
Eyes of aimed sperm and of egg on their errand,
Looking for immortality
In the lap of a broken volcano, in the furrow of a lost glacier,
Those shuttles of love-shadow?

Only humbler beings waved at me –
Weeds grazing the bottom, idling their tails.

Till the last pool –
A broad, coiling whorl, a deep ear
Of pondering amber,
Greenish and precious like a preservative,
With a ram's skull sunk there – magnified, a Medusa,
Funereal, phosphorescent, a lamp
Ten feet under the whisky.

I heard this pool whisper a warning.

I tickled its leading edges with temptation.
I stroked its throat with a whisker.
I licked the moulded hollows
Of its collarbones
Where the depth, now underbank opposite,
Pulsed up from contained excitements –

Eerie how you know when it's coming!
So I felt it now, my blood
Prickling and thickening, altering
With an ushering-in of chills, a weird onset
As if mountains were pushing mountains higher
Behind me, to crowd over my shoulder –

Then the pool lifted a travelling bulge
And grabbed the tip of my heart-nerve, and crashed,

Trying to wrench it from me, and again
Lifted a flash of arm for leverage

And it was a Gruagach of the Sligachan!
Some Boggart up from a crack in the granite!
A Glaistig out of the skull!

                – what was it gave me
Such a supernatural, beautiful fright

And let go, and sank disembodied
Into the eye-pupil darkness?

Only a little salmon.
              Salmo Salar
The loveliest, left-behind, most-longed-for ogress
Of the Palaeolithic
Watched me through her time-warped judas-hole
In the ruinous castle of Skye

As I faded from the light of reality.

Ophelia

Where the pool unfurls its undercloud –
There she goes.

And through and through
The kneading tumble and the water-hammer.

If a trout leaps into air, it is not for a breather.
It has to drop back immediately

Into this peculiar engine
That made it and keeps it going

And that works it to death –

                          there she goes
Darkfish, finger to her lips,
Staringly into the afterworld.

Creation of Fishes

All day
Sun burned among his burning brood
As all night
Moon flamed and her offspring spangled.

Under the Moon and her family
The souls of earthlings tried to hide in the sea.
Under the Sun and his family
Earth gaped: tongue and root shrivelled.

Said Moon to Sun: "Our children are too much
For this Creation. In their flame-beauty
They are too intolerably beautiful.
If the world is to live, they must be quenched."

Sun and Moon, solemn,
Gathered their children into a sack, to drown them.

Noble Sun, tear-blind, plucked his darlings.
Subtle Moon gathered glossy pebbles.

Both emptied their sack into the rivers.

Enraged, the hoodwinked Sun stared down, bereft.
Smiling, the Moon sloped away with her family.

The raving Sun fished up his loveliest daughter
To set her again beside him, in heaven,
But she spasmed, and stiffened, in a torture of colours.

He fished up his fieriest son who leaped
In agony from his hands, and plunged under.

He fished up his quickest, youngest daughter –
With dumb lips, with rigid working eye
She died in his fingers.

Flaring, his children fled through the river glooms.

Fingers dripping, the Sun wept in heaven.

Smiling, the Moon hid.

River Barrow

The light cools. Sun going down clear
Red-molten glass-blob, into green ember crumble
Of hill trees, over the Barrow
Where the flushed ash-grey sky lies perfect.

A skull tower is a nameless tomb. We sprawl
Rods out, giant grasshopper antennae, listening
For the bream-shoal to engage us.
                                    The current
Hauls its foam-line feed-lane
Along under the far bank – a furrow
Driving through heavy wealth,
Dragging a syrupy strength, a down-roping
Of the living honey.
                        It's an ancient thirst
Savouring all this, at the day's end,
Soaking it all up, through every membrane
As if the whole body were a craving mouth,
As if a hunted ghost were drinking – sud-flecks
Grass-bits and omens
Fixed in the glass.
                        Trees inverted
Even in this sliding place are perfect.
All evil suspended. Flies
Teem over my hands, twanging their codes
In and out of my ear's beam. Future, past,
Reading each other in the water mirror
Barely tremble the thick nerve.

56

                                    Heavy belly
Of river, solid mystery
With a living vein. Odd trout
Flash-plop, curdle the molten,
Rive a wound in the smooth healing.
Over the now pink-lit ballroom glass
Tiny sedge-flies partner their shadows.

A wobbly, wavering balance of light
Mercury precarious in its sac
Leans to the weir's edge, spilling. Dog-bark stillness.
A wood-pigeon is buffing the far edges
Of the smoothing peace.
                        Great weight
Resting effortless on the weightless.
A cow's moo moves through the complex
Of internestled metals, a moon-spasm
Through interfolded underseas. I lie here,
Half-unearthed, an old sword in its scabbard,
Happy to moulder. Only the river moves.

Feet prickling in my tight-sock gumboots,
Hair itching with midges, blood easy
As this river. Honeysuckle
Pouring its horns of plenty over us
From the thickets behind.
                            A big fish,
Bream-roll or evening salmon, crashes
A crater of suds, and the river widens.

A long-armed spider readjusts his gunsights
Between glumes of over-leaning river-grass.

Midge bites itching and swelling.

West Dart

It spills from the Milky Way, pronged with light,
It fuses the flash-gripped earth –

The spicy torrent, that seems to be water
Which is spirit and blood.

A violet glance of lightning
Melts the moorland to live glass,
Pours it into the mould of quick moor water

A trout swipes its flank at the thundercloud

A shatter of crowns, a tumbling out of goblets

Where the slag of world crumbles cooling
In thunders and rainy portents.

Strangers

Dawn. The river thins.
The combed-out coiffure at the pool-tail
Brightens thinly.
The slung pool's long hammock still flat out.

The sea-trout, a salt flotilla, at anchor,
Substanceless, flame-shadowed,
Hang in a near emptiness of sunlight.

There they actually are, under homebody oaks,
Close to teddybear sheep, near purple loose-strife –

Space-helms bowed in preoccupation,
Only a slight riffling of their tail-ailerons
Corrective of drift,
Gills easing.

And the pool's toiled rampart roots,
The cavorting of new heifers, water-skeeters
On their abacus, even the slow claim
Of the buzzard's hand
Merely decorate a heaven

Where the sea-trout, fixed and pouring,
Lean in the speed of light.
                              And make nothing
Of the strafed hogweed sentry skeletons,
Nothing of the sun, so openly aiming down.

Thistle-floss bowls over them. First, lost leaves
Feel over them with blind shadows.

The sea-trout, upstaring, in trance,
Absorb everything and forget it
Into a blank of bliss.

And this is the real samadhi – worldless, levitated.

Till, bulging, a man-shape
Wobbles their firmament.
                              Now see the holy ones
Shrink their auras, slim, sink, focus, prepare
To scram like trout.

After Moonless Midnight

I waded, deepening, and the fish
Listened for me. They watched my each move
Through their magical skins. In the stillness
Their eyes waited, furious with gold brightness,
Their gills moved. And in their thick sides
The power waited. And in their torpedo
Concentration, their mouth-aimed intent,
Their savagery waited, and their explosion.
They waited for me. The whole river
Listened to me, and, blind,
Invisibly watched me. And held me deeper
With its blind, invisible hands.
"We've got him," it whispered, "We've got him."

An August Salmon

Upstream and downstream, the river's closed.
Summer wastes in the pools.
A sunken calendar unfurls,
Fruit ripening as the petals rot.

A holed-up gangster,
He dozes, his head on the same stone,
Gazing towards the skylight,
Waiting for time to run out on him.

Alone, in a cellar of ashroots,
The bridegroom, mortally wounded
By love and destiny,
Features deforming with deferment.

His beauty bleeding invisibly
From every lift of his gills.

He gulps, awkward in his ponderous regalia,
But his eye stays rapt,
Elephantine, Arctic –
A god, on earth for the first time,
With the clock of love and death in his body.

Four feet under weightless, premature leaf-crisps
Stuck in the sliding sky. Sometimes
A wind wags a bramble up there.

The pulsing tiny trout, so separately fated,
Glue themselves to the stones near him.

His tail-frond, the life-root,
Fondling the poor flow, stays him
Sleeked ice, a smear of being
Over his anchor shadow.

Monkish, caressed
He kneels. He bows
Into the ceaseless gift
That unwinds the spool of his strength.

Dusk narrows too quickly. Manic depressive
Unspent, poltergeist anti-gravity
Spins him in his pit, levitates him
Through a fountain of plate glass,

Reveals his dragonized head,
The March-flank's ice-floe soul-flash
Rotted to a muddy net of bruise,
Flings his coil at the remainder of light –

Red-black and nearly unrecognizable,
He drops back, helpless with weight,
Tries to shake loose the riveted skull
And its ghoul decor –

sinks to the bed
Of his wedding cell, the coma waiting
For execution and death
In the skirts of his bride.

The Vintage of River is Unending

Grape-heavy woods ripen darkening
The sweetness.

Tight with golden light
The hills have been gathered.

Granite weights of sun.
Tread of burning days.

Unending river
Swells from the press
To gladden men.

Night Arrival of Seatrout

Honeysuckle hanging her fangs.
Foxglove rearing her open belly.
Dogrose touching the membrane.

Through the dew's mist, the oak's mass
Comes plunging, tossing dark antlers.

Then a shattering
Of the river's hole, where something leaps out –

An upside-down, buried heaven
Snarls, moon-mouthed, and shivers.

Summer dripping stars, biting at the nape.
Lobworms coupling in saliva.
Earth singing under her breath.

And out in the hard corn a horned god
Running and leaping
With a bat in his drum.

The Kingfisher

The Kingfisher perches. He studies.

Escaped from the jeweller's opium
X-rays the river's toppling
Tangle of glooms.

Now he's vanished – into vibrations.
A sudden electric wire, jarred rigid,
Snaps – with a blue flare.

He has left his needle buried in your ear.

Oafish oaks, kneeling, bend over
Dragging with their reflections
For the sunken stones. The Kingfisher
Erupts through the mirror, a shower of prisms –

A spilling armful of gems, beak full of ingots,
And is away – cutting the one straight line
Of the raggle-taggle tumbledown river
With a diamond –

Leaves a rainbow splinter sticking in your eye.

Through him, God, whizzing in the sun,
Glimpses the angler.

Through him, God
Marries a pit
Of fishy mire.
                    And look! He's
– gone again.
                    Spark, sapphire, refracted
From beyond water
Shivering the spine of the river.

That Morning

We came where the salmon were so many,
So steady, so spaced, so far-aimed
On their inner map, England could add

Only the sooty twilight of South Yorkshire
Hung with the drumming drift of Lancasters
Till the world had seemed capsizing slowly.

Solemn to stand there in the pollen light
Waist-deep in wild salmon swaying massed
As from the hand of God. There the body

Separated, golden and imperishable,
From its doubting thought – a spirit-beacon
Lit by the power of the salmon

That came on, came on, and kept on coming
As if we flew slowly, their formations
Lifting us toward some dazzle of blessing

One wrong thought might darken. As if the fallen
World and salmon were over. As if these
Were the imperishable fish

That had let the world pass away –

There in a mauve light of drifted lupins
They hung in the cupped hands of mountains

Made of tingling atoms. It had happened.
Then for a sign that we were where we were
Two gold bears came down and swam like men

Beside us. And dived like children.
And stood in deep water as on a throne
Eating pierced salmon off their talons.

So we found the end of our journey.

So we stood, alive in the river of light
Among the creatures of light, creatures of light.

River

Fallen from heaven, lies across
The lap of his mother, broken by world.

But water will go on
Issuing from heaven

In dumbness uttering spirit brightness
Through its broken mouth.

Scattered in a million pieces and buried
Its dry tombs will split, at a sign in the sky,

At a rending of veils.
It will rise, in a time after times,

After swallowing death and the pit
It will return stainless

For the delivery of this world.
So the river is a god

Knee-deep among reeds, watching men,
Or hung by the heels down the door of a dam

It is a god, and inviolable.
Immortal. And will wash itself of all deaths.

Last Night

The river seemed evil.
                    On the high fields, a full moon
Kept the world familiar. Moon-hazed
Hill over hill, the summer night
Turned on its pillow.
                    But down in the tree-cavern river,
The waded river, the river level with my knees,
The river under hangings of hemlock and nettle, and alder and oak,
Lay dark and grew darker. An evil mood
Darkened in it. Evil came up
Out of its stillest holes, and uncoiled
In the sick river, the drought river of slimes —
Like a sick man lying in the dark with his death.
Its darkness under roots, under old flood-battered boles
Was dark as blood,
Rusty peaty blood-dark, old-blood dark.
Something evil about the sunken river
In its sick-bed darkness. I stood in a grave
And felt the evil of fish. The strange evil
Of unknown fish-minds. Deep fish listening to me
In the dying river.

Gulkana

The Gulkana – where it meets the Copper –
Swung out of the black spruce forest, on a pebbly bend,
And disappeared into it,
Hazed with forest fires that had burned for weeks.

Strange word, "Gulkana". What did it mean?
A pre-Columbian glyph.
A pale, blue line, scrawled with a childish hand
Through our crumpled map. It was water
More than water, rocks that were more than rocks.

A scrapyard of boxy shacks
And supermarket refuse, dogs, wrecked pick-ups,
The Indian village where we bought our pass
Was comatose – on the stagnation toxins
Of a cultural vasectomy. They were relapsing
To Cloud-Like-A-Boulder, Mica, Bear, Magpie.

We hobbled along a tight-rope shore of pebbles
Under a trickling bluff
That bounced the odd pebble onto us, eerily.
(The whole land was in perpetual seismic tremor).
And the Gulkana
Biblical, a deranging cry
From the wilderness, burst past us –
A stone voice that dragged at us.
I found myself clinging
To the lifted horizon fringe of rag spruce

And the subsidence under my bootsoles
With balancing glances – nearly a fear,
Something I kept trying to deny

With deliberate steps. But it came with me
As if it swayed on my pack –
A nape of the neck unease. I'd sploshed far enough
Through the spongy sinks of the permafrost
For this river's
Miraculous fossils – creatures that each midsummer
Resurrected through it, in a fruit-sweet flesh.
Pilgrim for a fish!
Prospector for the lode in a fish's eye!

In the mercury light
My illusion developed. I felt hunted.
I tested my fear – it seemed to live in my neck,
A craven, bird-headed alertness.
And in my eyes
Which felt blind somehow to what I stared at
As if it stared at me. And in my ear –
So wary for the air-stir in the spruce-tips
My ear-drums almost ached. I explained it
To my quietly arguing, lucid panic
As my fear of one inside me,
A bodiless twin, some disinherited being
And doppelganger other, unliving,
Everliving, a larva from prehistory
Whose journey this was,
Whose gaze I could feel, who now exulted
Recognizing his home, and who watched me
Fiddling with my gear – the interloper,
The fool he had always hated. We pitched our tent

And for three days
Our tackle scratched the windows of the express torrent.
We seemed underpowered. Whatever we hooked
Bent in air, a small porpoise,
Then went straight downriver under the weight
And joined the Arctic landslide of the Copper
Which was the colour of cement.

Even when we got one ashore
It was too big to eat.

But there was the eye!
                          I peered into that lens
Seeking what I had come for. (What had I come for?
The camera-flash? The burned-out, staring bulb?)
What I saw was small, crazed, snake-like.
It made me think of a dwarf, sunken sun
And of the refrigerating pressures
Under the Bering Sea.

We relaunched the mulberry-dark torsos,
The gulping, sooted mouths, the glassy faces,

Arks of undelivered promise,
Egg-sacs of their own Eden —

Heavily veiled, seraphs of heavy ore
They surged away, magnetized
Into the furnace boom of the Gulkana.

Bliss had fixed their eyes
Like an anaesthetic.

They were possessed
By that voice in the river,
By the drums and flutes of its volume. We watched them
Move like drugged victims as they melted
Toward their sacrament – a consummation
Where only one thing was certain:
The actual, sundering death. The rebirth
Unknown, uncertain. Only that death
In the mercy of water, at the star of the source –

Devoured by revelation,
Every molecule seized, and tasted, and drained
Into the amethyst of emptiness –
I came back to myself.
                                        A spectre of fragments
Lifted my quivering coffee, in the aircraft,
And sipped at it.
I imagined our aircraft
As if a small boy held it
Making its noise. A spectre
Peered from the window, under the cobalt blaze,
Down onto Greenland's unremoving corpse
Tight-sheeted with snow-glare.
                                        Word by word
The burden of the river, beyond waking,
Numbed back into my marrow. While I recorded
The King Salmon's eye. And the blood-mote mosquito.
And the stilt-legged, one-rose rose
With its mock aperture, tilting toward us
In our tent-doorway, its needle tremor.

And the old Indian Headman, in his tatty jeans and socks, who smiled
Adjusting to our incomprehension – his face
A whole bat that glistened and stirred.

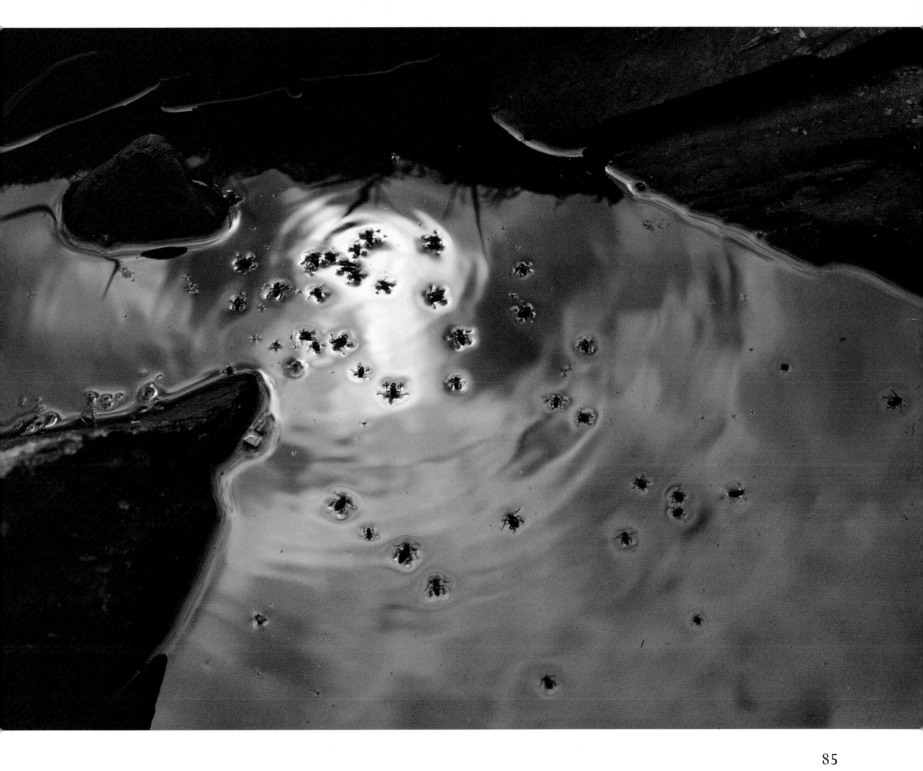

In the Dark Violin of the Valley

All night a music
Like a needle sewing body
And soul together, and sewing soul
And sky together and sky and earth
Together and sewing the river to the sea.

In the dark skull of the valley
A lancing, fathoming music
Searching the bones, engraving
On the draughty limits of ghost
In an entanglement of stars.

In the dark belly of the valley
A coming and going music
Cutting the bed-rock deeper

To earth-nerve, a scalpel of music

The valley dark rapt
Hunched over its river, the night attentive
Bowed over its valley, the river

Crying a violin in a grave
All the dead singing in the river

The river throbbing, the river the aorta

And the hills unconscious with listening.

Low Water

                                             This evening
The river is a beautiful idle woman.

The day's August burn-out has distilled
A heady sundowner.
She lies back. She is tipsy and bored.

She lolls on her deep couch. And a long thigh
Lifts from the flash of her silks.

Adoring trees, kneeling, ogreish eunuchs
Comb out her spread hair, massage her fingers.

She stretches – and an ecstasy tightens
Over her skin, and deep in her gold body

Thrills spasm and dissolve. She drowses.

Her half-dreams lift out of her, light-minded
Love-pact suicides. Copulation and death.

She stirs her love-potion – ooze of balsam
Thickened with fish-mucus and algae.

You stand under leaves, your feet in shallows.
She eyes you steadily from the beginning of the world.

A Rival

The cormorant, commissar of the hard sea,
Has not adjusted to the soft river.

He lifts his pterodactyl head in the drought pool
(Sound-proof cellar of final solutions).

The dinosaur massacre-machine
Hums on in his skull, programme unaltered.

That fossil eye-chip could reduce
All the blood in the world, yet still taste nothing.

At dawn he's at it, under the sick face —
Cancer in the lymph, uncontrollable.

Level your eye's aim and he's off
Knocking things over, out through the window —

An abortion-doctor
Black bag packed with vital organs

Dripping unspeakably.
                           Then away, heavy, high
Over the sea's iron curtain —

The pool lies there mutilated,
                                   face averted,
Dumb and ruined.

August Evening

Blue space burned out. Earth's bronzes cooling.
September
Edges this evening. Skyline trees hang charred.
The thistles
Survive a biological blaze – burnt splinters,
Skeletal carbons, crowned with ashes. The fuel
Nearly all gone.
                              And the river
Cools early, star-touched. New moon,
Not new leaf-curl tender, but crisp.
                                          Mist
Breathes on the sliding glass. The river
Still beer-tinted from the barley disaster
Is becoming wintry.
                        The sea-tribes are here,

They've come up for their weddings, their Michaelmas fair,
The carnival on the gravels.
                                    Wet fog midnight,
A sheathing sea-freeze, hardens round my head,
Stiffens my fingers. Oaks and alders
Fume to black blots opposite.
The river lifts to a ghostly trail of smoke.

Too serious to stir, the longships
Of the sea-trout
Secretive under the land's levels,
Holds crammed with religious purpose,
Cobble the long pod of winter.
They will not play tonight.

Their procession kneels, in God-hush.
Robed in the stilled flow of their Creator
They inhale unending. I share it a little.

Slowly their white pathway sinks from the world.

The river becomes terrible.

Climbing out, I make a silent third
With two owls reassuring each other.

Last Act

(performed by a male)

Just before the curtain falls in the river
The Damselfly, with offstage, inaudible shriek,
Reappears, weightless.

Hover-poised, in her snakeskin leotards,
A violet-dark elegance,

Eyelash-delicate, a dracula beauty,
In her acetylene jewels,

Her mascara smudged, her veils shimmer-fresh –

Late August. Some sycamore leaves
Already in their museum, eaten to lace.
Robin song bronze-touching the stillness
Over posthumous nettles. The swifts, as one,

Whipcracked, gone. Blackberries.
                              And now, lightly,
Adder-shock of this dainty assassin
Still in mid-passion –
                    still in her miracle-play:
Masked, archaic, mute, insect mystery
Out of the sun's crypt.

                    Everything is forgiven
Such a metamorphosis in love!
A Phaedra Titania
Dragon of crazed enamels!
Tragedienne of the ultra-violet,
So frail and so sulphurous,

Stepping so magnetically to her doom.

Lifted out of the river with tweezers
Dripping the sun's incandescence –
                              suddenly she
Switches her scene elsewhere.

      (Find him later, half way up a nettle,
      A touch-crumple petal of web and dew –
      Midget puppet-clown, tranced on his strings,
      In the nightfall pall of Balsam.)

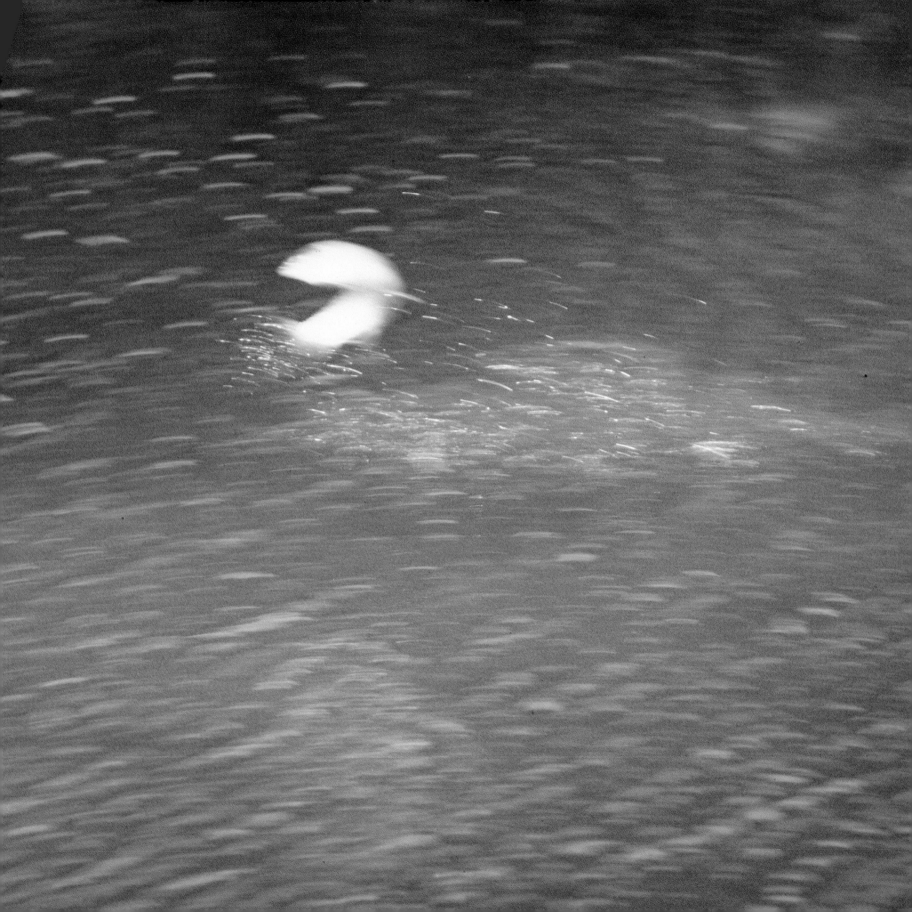

September Salmon

Famously home from sea,
Nobly preoccupied with his marriage licence,
He ignores the weir's wrangle. Ignores
The parochial downdrag
Of the pool's long diphthong. Ignores
Festivals of insect fluorescence.

He serves his descendants. And his homage
Is to be patient, performing, slowly, the palsy
Of concerted autumn
In the upside-down cage of a tree.

Does he envy the perennial eels and the mongrel minnows?
He is becoming a god,
A tree of sexual death, sacred with lichens.

Sometimes, for days, lost to himself.

                                        Mid-morning,
At the right angle of sun
You can see the floor of his chapel.
There he sways at the altar –
A soul
Hovering in the incantation and the incense.

Over his sky the skeeters traffic, godlike and double-jointed.
He lifts
To the molten palate of the mercurial light
And adds his daub.

Eighty and Still Fishing for Salmon

He holds
The loom of many rivers.
An old rowan now, arthritic, mossed,
Indifferent to man, roots for grave.

He's watching the Blackwater
Through Hotel glass. Estuary nets
Empty. The river fishless. He's a trophy
Of the Great Days – his wrinkles, his tweeds,

And that armchair. And the Tussaud stillness.
Probably he's being tossed
Across a Loch on Harris.
Both worlds have been lost

By the ritual mask
That hangs on its nail.
Soon he'll be out there, walking the sliding scree
Of the river – and over and over

His fly will come round on the vacant swirl.

An old Noh dancer, alone in the wind with his dance.
An air-fed, mountain prayer-wheel
Loyal to inbuilt bearings, touch of weather,
Now the heavens fail.

101

September

There's another river. In this river
Whose grandmotherly, earth-gnarled, sweetened hands
Welcome me with tremblings, give me the old feel
Of reality's reassurance –

There's a fishy nostalgia. The Balsam flower
Dangling loosely beside the gaze and pout,
Electric fingers parting a door curtain
Where smoky music shakes out.

An Eel

The strange part is his head. Her head. The strangely ripened
Domes over the brain, swollen nacelles
For some large containment. Lobed glands
Of some large awareness. Eerie the eel's head.
This full, plum-sleeked fruit of evolution.
Beneath it, her snout's a squashed slipper-face,
The mouth grin-long and perfunctory,
Undershot predatory. And the iris, dirty gold
Distilled only enough to be different
From the olive lode of her body,
The grained and woven blacks. And ringed larger
With a vaguer vision, an earlier eye
Behind her eye, paler, blinder,
Inward. Her buffalo hump
Begins the amazement of her progress.
Her mid-shoulder pectoral fin – concession
To fish-life – secretes itself
Flush with her concealing suit: under it
The skin's a pale exposure of deepest eel
As her belly is, a dulled pearl.
Strangest, the thumb-print skin, the rubberized weave
Of her insulation. Her whole body
Damascened with identity. This is she
Suspends the Sargasso
In her inmost hope. Her life is a cell
Sealed from event, her patience
Global and furthered with love
By the bending stars as if she
Were earth's sole initiate. Alone
In her millions, the moon's pilgrim,
The nun of water.

Fairy Flood

A brown musically-moving beauty, the earth's fullness
Slides towards the sea. An escape
Of earth-serpent, with all its hoards, casting the land, like
                                    an old skin,
Pulling its body from under the eye.

                                   Escaping daughter
Her whole glass castle melting about her
In full magic –

Some mask of crumpling woe disfigures
Her deep liberation, which is actually jubilant,
As she brings down earth and sky blamelessly
In this headlong elopement without finery,
Weeps past – a freed out-heaping
Of accusative love and abandon.

The fatherly landscape upbraids and harangues,
Claws weakly at her swollen decision
With gaping beard and disarrayed robe,
Undoes his stained bandages,
Exposes him bone-open wounds –

The river cries out once, tosses her hair, hides her eyes,
Bleeding him empty remorselessly.

Riverwatcher

How easy the moist flash, the long eye-slit,
The river's polished key-hole
Opens to ghost – a holy fool
In the bauble mosque of the skull!

O birdwatcher, sit brambly still
Till wrens alight on you, O twilit angler
Tucked in your blood-knot, lift off deftly
As a sedge-fly, keep your head clear

Of the river-fetch –

                              (the epileptic's strobe,
The yell of the Muezzin
Or the "Bismillah!"
That spins the dancer in

Her whole body liquefied
Where a body loves to be
Rapt in the river of its own music) –

With dry difficulty

Cling to the gnat, the dead leaf
In the riding whorls
That loosen and melt
Into the bellies of pools.

October Salmon

He's lying in poor water, a yard or so depth of poor safety,
Maybe only two feet under the no-protection of an outleaning small oak,
Half-under a tangle of brambles.

After his two thousand miles, he rests,
Breathing in that lap of easy current
In his graveyard pool.

About six pounds weight,
Four years old at most, and hardly a winter at sea —
But already a veteran,
Already a death-patched hero. So quickly it's over!

So briefly he roamed the gallery of marvels!
Such sweet months, so richly embroidered into earth's beauty-dress,
Her life-robe —
Now worn out with her tirelessness, her insatiable quest,
Hangs in the flow, a frayed scarf —

An autumnal pod of his flower,
The mere hull of his prime, shrunk at shoulder and flank,

With the sea-going Aurora Borealis of his April power —
The primrose and violet of that first upfling in the estuary —
Ripened to muddy dregs,
The river reclaiming his sea-metals.

In the October light
He hangs there, patched with leper-cloths.

Death has already dressed him
In her clownish regimentals, her badges and decorations,
Mapping the completion of his service,
His face a ghoul-mask, a dinosaur of senility, and his whole body
A fungoid anemone of canker —

Can the caress of water ease him?
The flow will not let up for a minute.

What a change! from that covenant of Polar Light
To this shroud in a gutter!
What a death-in-life — to be his own spectre!
His living body become death's puppet,
Dolled by death in her crude paints and drapes
He haunts his own staring vigil
And suffers the subjection, and the dumbness,
And the humiliation of the role!

And that is how it is,
That is what is going on there, under the scrubby oak tree, hour after hour,
That is what the splendour of the sea has come down to,
And the eye of ravenous joy — king of infinite liberty
In the flashing expanse, the bloom of sea-life,

On the surge-ride of energy, weightless,
Body simply the armature of energy
In that earliest sea-freedom, the savage amazement of life,
The salt mouthful of actual existence
With strength like light —

Yet this was always with him. This was inscribed in his egg.
This chamber of horrors is also home.
He was probably hatched in this very pool.

And this was the only mother he ever had, this uneasy channel of minnows
Under the mill-wall, with bicycle wheels, car-tyres, bottles
And sunk sheets of corrugated iron.
People walking their dogs trail their evening shadows across him.
If boys see him they will try to kill him.

All this, too, is stitched into the torn richness,
The epic poise
That holds him so steady in his wounds, so loyal to his doom, so patient
In the machinery of heaven.

Visitation

All night the river's twists
Bit each other's tails, in happy play.

Suddenly a dark other
Twisted in among them.

And a cry, half sky, half bird,
Slithered over roots.
                    A star
Fleetingly etched it.

                    Dawn
Puzzles a sunk branch under deep tremblings.

Nettles will not tell.
                    Who shall say
That the river
Crawled out of the river, and whistled,
And was answered by another river?

A strange tree
Is the water of life –

Sheds these pad-clusters on mud-margins
One dawn in a year, her eeriest flower.

Torridge

Which ones
Of the eager faces, garlic or iris
Come back for the new herons?

Once the floods have wiped away their pollen
Have undressed them
And folded them into winter?

Venus and Jupiter, year in and year out
Contend for the crown
Of morning star and of evening star.

And the fish worship the source, bowed and fervent,
But their hearts are water.

The river walks in the valley singing
Letting her veils blow –

A novelty from the red side of Adam.

April in the lift of her arm
December in the turn of her shoulder

As if her sauntering were a long stillness.

She who has not once tasted death.

Salmon Eggs

The salmon were just down there –
Shuddering together, touching each other,
Emptying themselves for each other –

Now beneath flood-murmur
They curve away deathwards.

                                        January haze,
With a veined yolk of sun. In bone-damp cold
I lean and watch the water, listening to water
Till my eyes forget me

And the piled flow supplants me, the mud-blooms

All this ponderous light of everlasting
Collapsing away under its own weight

Mastodon ephemera

Mud-curdling, bull-dozing, hem-twinkling
Caesarian of heaven and earth, unfelt

With exhumations and delirious advents –

                                        Catkins

Wriggle at their mother's abundance. The spider clings to his craft.

Something else is going on in the river

More vital than death – death here seems a superficiality
Of small scaly limbs, parasitical. More grave than life
Whose reflex jaws and famished crystals
Seem incidental
To this telling – these toilings of plasm –
The melt of mouthing silence, the charge of light
Dumb with immensity.

            The river goes on
Sliding through its place, undergoing itself
In its wheel.

        I make out the sunk foundations
Of burst crypts, a bedrock
Time-hewn, time-riven altar. And this is the liturgy
Of the earth's tidings – harrowing, crowned – a travail
Of raptures and rendings.

            Sanctus Sanctus
Swathes the blessed issue.

           Perpetual mass
Of the waters
Wells from the cleft.

          It is the swollen vent
Of the nameless
Teeming inside atoms – and inside the haze
And inside the sun and inside the earth.

It is the font, brimming with touch and whisper
Swaddling the egg.

Only birth matters
Say the river's whorls.

And the river
Silences everything in a leaf-mouldering hush
Where sun rolls bare, and earth rolls,

And mind condenses on old haws.

Notes on the Photographs

A rare sight: a jumping sea-trout on the Welsh Dovey. 97
Often these leaps from the water are not actions of pure
pleasure but have the more practical purpose of ridding the
fish of sea-lice.

Tell-tale rings of rising fish form a decorative pattern on 99
a broad sweep of the Bundorragha river, County Mayo.

The Scottish Dee has been called 'the river flowing out 101
of Paradise'. A British Gas pipeline crosses the Dee,
unseen and unheard, at this point.

A salmon, undisturbed by the large gas pipeline in the 103
river bed, moves in a pool on the river Don. British Gas,
in close consultation with river authorities, has crossed
many rivers in bringing the pipeline southwards.

Delicately balanced craneflies mate in the long riverside 105
grasses.

Speckled brown trout lie in a sunlit pool on the 107
Hampshire Test.

The river Dart is infinitely variable during its course to 109
the sea, flowing through deep pools and over shallow runs
between rocks.

Late autumn on the Devonshire Dart and the 111
golden-brown beech leaves seem reluctant to fall.

On the way to the breeding reeds at the headwaters of 113
the river Feugh, a salmon takes on the fury of a late
autumn spate.

Autumnal beads of dew cling to a spiders web, 115
emphasising its intricate and sinister pattern.

A cow parsley seedhead with hoarfrost completes the 117
seasons' cycle with a return to winter.

At the water's edge ice crystals and miniature chasms 119
are formed as freezing and thawing alternate.

A quieter breeding ground for salmon and sea-trout. 121
The Devonshire Lyd in winter above Hartley weir.

The red of winter, a hawthorn berry with raindrop. 123

The river Exe at a British Gas pipeline crossing. In this 125
case, as with all other river crossings, no scars are evident
in the landscape and great care is taken not to disturb the
life-cycle of the river bed.